This book belongs to:

_____

_____

I am incredibly grateful for your purchase, and I want to thank you.

I hope you enjoyed coloring this book, and it makes me happy knowing that it brought a tiny bit of delight in your everyday life.

If you found some benefit in this book, I would appreciate hearing from you and hope that you can take some time to post a review.

Your review is very important for me as an author, as it will improve the creation of future books, and it will also help other readers to discover this book.

You can also contact me at stefanheartpress@gmail.com

www.ingramcontent.com/pod-product-compliance
Lightning Source LLC
Chambersburg PA
CBHW082040080526
44578CB00009B/786